Wild Turkeys

Julian May
Wild Turkeys

Pictures by John Hamberger

Holiday House • New York

Text copyright © 1973 by Julian May Dikty
Illustrations copyright © 1973 by John Hamberger
All rights reserved
Printed in the United States of America
Library of Congress catalog card number: 72-92582
ISBN 0-8234-0217-7

The Pilgrims of Plymouth Colony had a lot to be thankful for in the autumn of 1621. Friendly Indians had shown them how to plant corn. They would not starve, as they had during the terrible winter of 1620. When the harvest was ready, the Pilgrims called the Indians to a great feast— the first Thanksgiving meal. One of the dishes served was roast wild turkey.

The American colonies became the United States.
People remembered the Pilgrims and celebrated
Thanksgiving Day. Whenever they could, they ate roast
turkey at their feast. The beautiful, big bird had become
the symbol of Thanksgiving. It still is today.

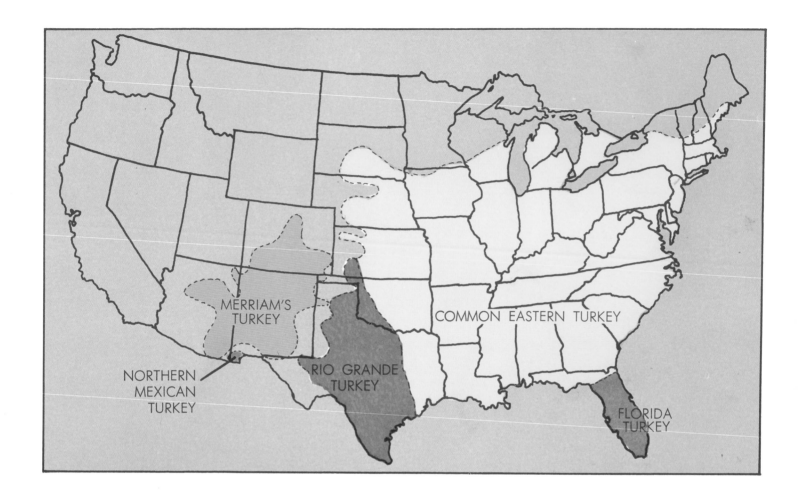

Wild turkeys are found only in the New World. They are relatives
of chickens and pheasants. Besides the common turkey,
which once ranged all over the eastern United States and
southern Ontario, there were several other breeds,
such as the Florida turkey and the Rio Grande turkey.
A completely different bird, the ocellated turkey, inhabited
the jungles of Guatemala and Yucatan.

The wild turkey is a beautiful bird with a slender body
and long, strong legs. The male, called a gobbler or tom,
has brilliant feathers—coppery bronze with many
black and brown bands. When the bird is in the sun, its
feathers give off metallic reflections of green, purple
and copper. An odd tuft of hairy feathers, the "beard,"
hangs from the male's upper breast.

The females, called hens, are smaller than the males and have less colorful feathers. They sometimes have a beard. Strange folds of skin decorate a turkey's bare head. Above the beak is a fleshy dewbill; below it hang wattles. Males, especially, can change the head color rapidly from blue to red or orange. They also swell up the skin folds as they change moods.

Early in spring, as the sun rises, each male turkey begins to stir. All night long he has roosted on a tree branch, shoulders hunched up to keep his bare head warm. The break of day is the signal for him to begin seeking a mate. He flies to the ground and utters his mating call: *gil-obble-obble-obble quit quit cut!*

Again and again he gobbles. Finally there is a shy
answer: *kee-e-ow, kee-e-ow, kee-e-ow.* A turkey hen
peeps out from among the bushes. The gobbler struts
before her, his tail feathers spread out like
a glittering fan, his wings dragging on the ground.
Taking in a great gulp of air, he inflates his body.
The feathers fluff out and he seems very large and
handsome. *Puff! Cluck! Vroom!* He lets the air escape.

Sometimes two males fight over a strutting-ground.
But most strutting sessions are peaceful. The gobbler
works very hard to gather a group of two to five hens,
who visit him daily and mate with him. After the mating
season is over, he is worn out. He goes off to live
quietly with other males.

ROBIN CHICKEN TURKEY

Turkeys are not very intelligent birds. However,
most wild hens are smart enough to make their nests
where animal enemies cannot find them. The usual nest is
a shallow hole scooped out of the earth and padded with
leaves. The hen lays four to sixteen white or buff eggs;
they may also have speckles. When she has to leave the nest,
she covers them up. After 28 days, the young, called
poults, are hatched.

Like baby chicks, the turkey poults have open eyes, a fluffy coat of down, and an alert manner. They begin running about the nest shortly after hatching. Clucking softly, the mother leads them out into the forest to look for food. She does not have to teach the little ones to scratch and peck at the ground in search of insects.

If danger threatens, the mother may pretend to be crippled—luring the enemy away while the young crouch motionless on the forest floor. Because of their color, the poults are almost invisible when they are hiding. Crows, owls, and hawks are among the most important enemies of wild turkeys. Four-footed animals have a hard time catching turkeys. The birds can run at more than 18 miles an hour and can fly nearly 55 miles an hour for short distances.

For the first two weeks of life, the poults must be
kept warm and dry. If it should rain, the mother shelters
her brood under her wings. If they become soaked, they
are likely to die. Young birds are unable to stand cold
temperatures either, and it is this that prevents wild
turkeys from living in places with long, cold winters.

The poults grow very quickly, and as they do they molt, or shed their old feathers. Later new ones grow in. The babies have fluffy pinkish-tan down, streaked and speckled with brown. At six weeks of age they have a full coat of speckled feathers. In fall they grow a darker coat and their heads have a strange fuzzy or mossy covering that later falls out. By spring the young birds have adult feathers.

Besides eating insects—especially grasshoppers—wild turkeys are very fond of acorns and other seeds. One part of the bird's stomach, the gizzard, is able to crush and grind up the toughest nutshell in a short time. As autumn comes, the birds feed on many fruits and berries. During the winter they scratch through the snow or eat the buds from trees and shrubs.

For thousands of years the Indians of North America and
Mexico hunted wild turkeys for food. They also used the
birds' feathers for ornamental headdresses, skirts,
and cloaks. The birds were wary and had to be hunted skillfully.
Sometimes they were shot with arrows vaned with turkey feathers.
Turkey eggs too are delicious, and the Indians ate them
whenever they could be found.

The Indians learned how to tame turkeys a long time ago. They caught young birds, clipped their wing feathers so they could not fly, and kept them in pens. Mexican Indians did this at least 2000 years ago. Slowly these captive turkeys became domesticated—they lost their desire to fly away into the wilds and were content to live with man.

Domestic turkeys, herded like sheep, were common in Mexico
and the American Southwest about the year 700. Spanish explorers
discovered both the Indians and their domestic birds. The
first turkeys were sent to Spain about 1511 and from there
to England in about 1541. Because they were so large and
so good to eat, turkeys were sent all over Europe. They
were common at English Christmas feasts about 1575.

Domestic turkeys returned to America in 1607, when English colonists came to Virginia. Some of the tame birds escaped and mated with the wild gobblers. The mixed offspring were often larger than their parents. Settlers hunted the wild turkeys so eagerly that they began to become rare. The first law to protect the birds was signed in New York in 1708.

As more and more people came to live in America, the vast forests that the eastern Indians knew were chopped down by white farmers. There was less room for wild turkeys. Men continued to hunt them. And some greedy hunters killed more turkeys than they could possibly eat. Man's dogs, cats, and hogs attacked wild turkey eggs and poults. By the early 1900s, wild turkeys had begun to disappear from places where they were once common.

BOURBON RED

WHITE HOLLAND

BLACK

The American appetite for turkey meat has remained as strong as ever. Farmers raised domestic birds, beginning in early colonial times. They bred many new varieties by crossing wild birds with the old domestic type. Some modern domestic breeds are very large—with toms weighing more than 40 pounds.

BELTSVILLE WHITE

BRONZE

NARRAGANSETT

It is not easy to raise turkeys successfully. The young
birds may die during bad weather. Both young and adults
easily become diseased. And turkeys are likely to
stampede if they are frightened, leaving many birds injured
or dead. Nonetheless, millions of turkeys are raised each
year in the United States and Canada—and in many other
countries of the world as well.

As years passed, the real wild turkey became scarce or
even extinct in most of the eastern United States. From
time to time people tried to restock the forests with
turkeys raised in game farms. But many of these birds had
descended from domestic turkeys. When they were set free they proved
to be slower and less intelligent than true wild birds.
Foxes, skunks, and raccoons destroyed the poorly hidden
eggs and young. The adults were likely to roost near
farmhouses, where they were easily shot.

Wildlife workers learned that only true wild turkeys would
survive when they were set free. They learned that turkeys would
not thrive in places that had cold, wet springtimes or
in places where the summers were very hot and dry. Today
the number of wild turkeys is slowly increasing.

In a few states, wild turkeys are so numerous that people are allowed to hunt them. Most wild turkeys in the United States are found in Texas, Florida, Alabama, Arizona, Pennsylvania, New Mexico, Georgia, and Mississippi. If we want to have more of these magnificent birds, we must be willing to set aside forests and other wild areas where turkeys and other animals will be able to feed and raise their young in peace.